saraswathi editions
Cochin, India

Kohinoor of
Rice and Spice

ISBN: 81-7436-254-1

© **Roli & Janssen BV 2003**
Published in India by Roli Books
in arrangement with Roli & Janssen
M-75 Greater Kailash-II (Market)
New Delhi 110 048, India.
Phone: 6442271, 6462782 Fax: 6467185
Email: roli@vsnl.com Website: rolibooks.com

Printed and bound at Singapore

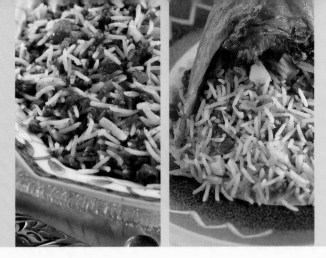

Kohinoor of
Rice and Spice

Text: Rocky Mohan

Photos: Siddharth Mishra

Rocky Mohan
. c o o k e r y   c l u b .
Roli Books

Contents

THE ORIGIN OF RICE

Rice is probably the most significant and important cereal in the world. Its origin and history is obscure, but it is known to have been the staple food for eons and is so for more than half the world's population.

Oryza Sativa, it is believed, is associated with wet, humid climate, though it is not a tropical plant. It is probably a descendent of wild grass that was most likely cultivated in the foothills of the far Eastern Himalayas, and in the upper areas of the Irrawady and Mekong.

Another school of thought believes that the rice plant may have originated in southern India, then spread to the north of the country and then onwards to China. It then arrived in Korea, the Philippines (about 2000 B.C.) and then Japan and Indonesia (about 1000 B.C.). The Persians are known to have been importers of this grain to Mesopotamia and Turkestan. When Alexander the Great invaded India in 327 B.C., it is believed that he took rice back to Greece.

Arab travellers took it to Egypt, Morocco and Spain and that is how it travelled all across Europe. Portugal and Holland took rice to their colonies in West Africa and then it travelled to America through the 'Columbian Exchange' of natural resources, rice being a gift from the Old World to the New. But as is traditionally known, rice is a slow starter and this is also true to the fact that it took close to two centuries after the voyages of Columbus for rice to take root in the Americas. Thereafter, the journey of rice continues with the Moors taking it to Spain in A.D. 700 and then the Spanish brought rice to South America at the beginning of the seventeenth century.

The journey of rice around the world has been slow, but once it took root it stayed and became a major agricultural and economic product for the people. In the Indian subcontinent more than a quarter of the cultivated land is given to rice. It is a very essential part of the daily meal in the southern and eastern parts of India. In the northern and central parts of the subcontinent, where breads are frequently eaten, rice holds its own and is cooked daily as well as on festivals and special occasions.

The rice grain is treated with honour in the subcontinent and in Asia as well; for here the failure of the rice crop in not only an economic setback but can create a famine-like situation. Wastage of rice is viewed rather badly in these societies and superstitions to this effect are also attached to this.

VARIETIES AND TYPES

There are over 100,000 or more varieties of rice of which some 8,000 are cultivated by man for food. The rest are 'wild rices' but they must not be mistaken with the long, black grains of wild rice, which is a different plant altogether.

There are three main types of rice:

* The 6-mm long grain, which when cooked, remains separate.
* The 5-6-mm medium grain, is a little shorter than the long-grain rice and this variety remains firm and light when cooked but does tend to stick when cooled.
* The 4-5-mm short grain, with round grains, tends to stick together when cooked. There are a number of intermediate types as well. The classification is according to the type of mechanical or physical processing the grain receives after harvesting.

Paddy Rice: Is un-husked rice in its raw state, with no further treatment after threshing.

Brown Rice: Also called *'cargo rice'*, as this rice was transported in cargo ships from the Far East to Europe. It has a characteristic beige colour and is the most nutritious form of rice; its nutty flavour is rather strong.

White Rice: Is brown rice from which the germ and outer layer of pericap have been removed. It is also called *unpolished rice.*

Polished Rice: Is white rice, which has been hulled and polished. In some countries it is enriched with metals and vitamins in order to restore some of its nutritional value. The polishing is done to give the grain a shining whiter look.

Glacé Rice: Is polished rice covered with a fine coat of French chalk suspended in a glucose mix and then processed to give it an attractive sheen.

Steamed Pre-treated Rice: Is paddy rice that has been carefully cleaned, soaked in hot water, steamed at a low pressure and then de-husked and blanched.

Pre-cooked Rice: Is rice that has been husked, blanched and soaked, boiled for 2-3 minutes and then dried at 200°C / 400°F. It is popular in France.

Camolino Rice: Is polished rice that is lightly coated with oil.

Puffed Rice: In India it is roasted on hot sand, while in the USA it is treated with heat at high pressure and then at low pressure.

Wild Rice: Is the seed of a water grass, though related to the rice plant. It grows one seed by one seed up the stalk of the plant. It is very expensive and is some times mixed with brown rice.

Indian Basmati Rice: Indian Basmati is aromatic rice, but has a very different aroma and taste from Thai Jasmine rice or other perfumed rice. Some describe its aroma as popcorn like. This rice is grown in the northern Punjab region of India and Pakistan, and commands the highest price of any variety of rice grown in the world. (Not counting artificially high prices for rice in Japan.) This rice has high amylase content and a firm almost dry texture when properly cooked. The raw kernel is long and slender like southern long-grain rice, but slightly smaller. The kernels increase in length by more than two and a half times when cooked to produce a very long slender cooked grain. The best Indian Basmati has been aged for at least one year to increase firmness of cooked texture and the elongation achieved in cooking. Once again, there are many 'knock off' varieties grown in the US, but none match the authentic Indian Basmati for flavour, aroma, texture, and appearance.

Surinam Rice: A rice sought after by connoisseurs, has very long, thin grains and is native to Surinam.

Perfumed Rice: This long-grained rice comes from Thailand and Vietnam and has a very distinctive taste. Mostly served at feasts or on very special occasions.

Sticky Rice: Is long-grained, and is high on starch content. It is rarely available. Best suited for Chinese cuisine.

Carolina Rice: Thomas Jefferson travelled to Piedmont to find out why Italian rice fetched a higher price than Carolina rice and to improve the product genetically he smuggled a seed out in his pocket. But the name is no longer used to describe a particular variety.

Popped Rice: Is heated to 200°C in oil and resembles popcorn.

Rice Flakes: Is steamed husked rice, flattened into thin flakes, eaten at breakfast with milk and sugar or as a savoury snack fried and tossed with salt and spices.

PREPARING

Medium and round-grain rice should be washed before cooking to keep them from sticking. Rinse the rice under cold running water until the water is clear. Basmati rice (other perfumed rices) must be soaked in cold water before being cooked. Add rice to cold water in a bowl and stir. Replace the water when it turns milky and repeat this process until the water is clear. Rinsing the rice prior to cooking gives it a lighter, less creamy texture.

COOKING

Rice can be boiled in water, stock, juice, milk, yoghurt or coconut milk, according to different methods:

✳ Basmati rice is delicate, perfumed and aromatic, and requires less cooking liquid. It must be cooked over very low heat after achieving a rapid boil in the beginning. For pre-soaked rice it is suggested that 1¼ cups of liquid be used for 1 cup of rice; while 1½ cups of liquid be used if the rice is not pre-soaked. To soak, use 2 cups of cold water for 1 cup of rice for

30 minutes. Then drain the rice and let it stand for 10 minutes before cooking. Pour the rice into a saucepan, add the right quantity of liquid and bring to the boil, reduce heat and then cook, covered, over very low heat for 20 minutes. Turn off the heat and let the rice stand for 10 minutes.

✳ Use 1 cup of rice with 2 cups of liquid. Place the liquid and rice in a pot and bring to the boil; lower heat, cover, and then simmer gently until all the liquid is absorbed. Alternatively bring the liquid to the boil and then add the rice and simmer until the liquid is absorbed.

✳ Add the rice to a large quantity of boiling water, bring back to the boil, lower heat and cook until the rice is of the right consistency; drain. To further reduce the moisture dry the rice in the oven at 250°C for 10-12 minutes.

✳ Brown rice needs to be soaked in water for 1 hour and then cooked in the same water for 40-45 minutes.

✳ Wash the rice as described above for *Basmati rice*. Then place the rice in a pan and cover with cold water. Cover the pan and bring to the boil over high heat, reduce heat to medium and cook until small craters are formed on the surface. Lower heat further and simmer, covered, for 15 minutes. Care must be taken not to overcook the rice, as this will make it stick to the bottom of the pan.

The cooking time varies depending on the type of rice being cooked and on individual preference.
The cooking times given are approximate:
Parboiled rice 25 minutes; white rice 15 minutes; brown rice 45 minutes; and instant rice 5 minutes.

GUIDELINES FOR BOILING RICE

✳ For firm rice, reduce the quantity of liquid.
✳ For soft rice, use a little more liquid.
✳ If the rice is to be served later, reduce the cooking time to allow the rice to cook when re-heated. If liquid is left after the rice is cooked, remove the cover and increase the heat to

evaporate the extra liquid. If too much liquid remains when the rice is cooked, drain it and use the liquid to make soups, sauces or stews. Do not stir the rice excessively during the cooking process and specially once the rice is cooked, as this will break the grains.

GUIDELINES FOR STEAMING RICE

Put a double boiler over boiling water and pour the rice into the top of the boiler. Cover the double boiler and simmer over medium heat. Heat the fat and then add the washed/soaked rice. Mix well coating the grains with the fat. Add double the volume in liquid, cover the pan and simmer until the liquid is absorbed. Rice cooked in this manner remains firm and does not stick.

GUIDELINES FOR STORING RICE

* Brown rice contains the rich germ and should be stored in an airtight container in a refrigerator to avoid it going rotten and to prevent the absorption of odours.
* White rice should be stored in a cool, dry place, which is insect free.
* Cooked rice is highly perishable and will keep for a few days in the refrigerator, if stored in a covered container. However, it can be frozen for 6-8 months.

NUTRITIONAL INFORMATION

per 100 gm	long-grain cooked brown rice	long-grain cooked white rice
Protein	2.6 gm	2.7 gm
Fat	0.9 gm	0.3 gm
Carbohydrates	23 gm	27 gm
Fibre	1.7 gm	0.4 gm
Water	73%	68.7%

INDIAN SPICES AND CONDIMENTS

Spices are the very heart and soul of Indian cuisine. They form the foundation of a cuisine that has existed for centuries. It is virtually impossible to cook Indian dishes without spices, even if they are only red chillies and salt.

1. **Bay leaves (*tej patta*):** An aromatic herb used for flavouring vegetables and meat.
2. **Black peppercorns (*sabut kali mirch*):** A pungent aromatic condiment.
3. **Cardamoms (*elaichi*):** One of the world's most expensive spices, there are two varieties – the large, black-brown ones, which have a heavier flavour and the small green ones which are aromatic and have a delicate flavour.
4. **Carom seeds (*ajwain*):** Also known as thymol or omum; used in pickles and vegetable dishes.
5. **Chilli and chilli powder:** There are at least 20 known varieties of chilli powders. The range of chillies can be from white and yellow to saffron and red in colour. While capsicums or peppers are mild and flavoured, Goan chillies are dark red in colour and not pungent. Green chillies are similar to fresh red chillies and their seeds are the most pungent. Red Kashmiri chillies are very mild and can be used for colouring and flavouring.
6. **Cinnamon (*dalchini*):** Most Indian food is cooked with cassia bark, which is a good substitute for real cinnamon. However, it does not have the delicate flavour of cinnamon as its flavour is much stronger.
7. **Cloves (*laung*):** Cloves are the dried flower buds of an evergreen plant. The oil of cloves contains phenol, which is a good antiseptic and helps in preserving food.
8. **Coriander (*dhaniya*) seeds:** Coriander seed powder is a very important spice in Indian food. Fresh coriander leaves are used for garnishing. Coriander has a strong, pungent smell but is almost indispensable to Indian cuisine.

9. **Cumin (*jeera*) seeds:** Cumin seeds come in two varieties: white and black. The white variety is the more common one and is used as extensively as coriander seed powder, while the black variety is more aromatic and peppery.

10. **Curry leaves (*kadhi patta*):** These impart a subtle flavour when fried until they are crisp. They are popular in South Indian dishes.

11. **Fennel (*moti saunf*) seeds:** Fennel seeds are a common ingredient for flavouring stocks, sauces, and curries. Used extensively as an ingredient in *paan* and as an effective digestive.

12. **Fenugreek seeds (*methi dana*):** Fenugreek seeds are square, flat and yellowish-brown in colour. Care must be taken in using the seeds as they are bitter and the quantity used must be controlled.

13. **Mace (*javitri*):** Mace is a part of the nutmeg. It is the shell of the nutmeg kernel. It has a flavour similar to nutmeg, but is more delicate and is used in rice dishes.

14. **Mustard seeds (*rai*):** Tiny, dark, round seeds used for tempering in dals and pickles.

15. **Nutmeg (*jaiphal*):** This is used to make fragrant garam masala. The kernel must be finely grated just before use. Excessive use must be avoided as it can be poisonous.

16. **Onion seeds (*kalonji*):** Sprinkled over Indian breads and used in cooking vegetables.

17. **Pomegranate seeds (*anar dana*):** Used in making savouries, and for giving a sour flavour.

18. **Poppy (*khuskhus*) seeds:** White poppy seeds, roasted and ground, are used to provide a nutty flavour and to thicken gravies.

19. **Saffron (*kesar*):** The world's most expensive spice, saffron must be soaked in either warm milk or water and used at the end of cooking a dish.

20. **Tamarind (*imli*):** The bitter-sweet, highly acidic pulp of the tamarind is used to flavour foods, and is a good source of iron, potassium and magnesium.

21. **Turmeric (*haldi*):** Turmeric is a rhizome of the ginger family.

BASIC RECIPES

Making masalas at home is an essential part of the Indian cuisine. Here are some recipes you will find very useful.

Standard Garam Masala

Ingredients:

4 tbsp / 24 gm	Black cumin *(shah jeera)* seeds	4 tbsp / 40	Green cardamom *(choti elaichi)* seeds
4 tbsp / 24 gm	Cumin *(jeera)* seeds	6	Cinnamon *(dalchini)* sticks, 1" each
4 tbsp / 40	Cloves *(laung)*	2 tbsp / 25	Black peppercorns *(sabut kali mirch)*
12	Bay leaves *(tej patta)*	½tsp / 1 gm	Mace *(javitri)*, powdered
4 tbsp / 40	Black cardamom *(bari elaichi)* seeds	2 tbsp / 9 gm	Dry ginger powder *(sonth)*

Method: Dry roast the black cumin seeds, cumin seeds, cloves, bay leaves, black cardamom seeds, green cardamom seeds, cinnamon sticks, and black peppercorns on low heat until aromatic. Remove from heat and cool. Put all the roasted spices, mace and dry ginger powder in an electric blender and grind to a fine powder. Then pass the powder through a fine sieve. Store in an airtight container.

Fragrant Garam Masala

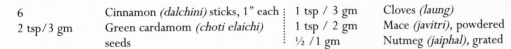

Ingredients:

6	Cinnamon *(dalchini)* sticks, 1" each	1 tsp / 3 gm	Cloves *(laung)*
2 tsp/3 gm	Green cardamom *(choti elaichi)* seeds	1 tsp / 2 gm	Mace *(javitri)*, powdered
		½ /1 gm	Nutmeg *(jaiphal)*, grated

Method: Dry roast the cinnamon sticks, green cardamom seeds, cloves, and mace powder on low heat until aromatic. Mix the dry, roasted spices with the grated nutmeg and blend to make a fine powder. Then follow the same method as mentioned for the Standard Garam Masala.

Kashmiri Garam Masala

Ingredients:

4 tsp / 6 gm	Green cardamom *(choti elaichi)* seeds	2 tsp /12 gm	Black peppercorns *(sabut kali mirch)*
2 tsp / 3 gm	Black cumin *(shah jeera)* seeds	1 tsp / 3 gm	Cloves *(laung)*
6	Cinnamon *(dalchini)* sticks, 1" each	½ / 1 gm	Nutmeg *(jaiphal)*, grated

Method: Use the same method as for the Standard and Fragrant garam masalas.

Cooked Yoghurt

Whisk 2 cups yoghurt until smooth. Add ½ cup water and whisk again. Cook on high heat till the mixture comes to the boil. Lower heat, cook till the mixture is reduced to ½ and the colour changes to off-white. Use as specified in the recipe.

Keema Ki Biryani

Royal mince biryani

Serves: 4

Ingredients:

2 cups / 400 gm	Basmati rice, washed, soaked in water for 1 hour, drained
500 gm	Lamb, minced
½ cup / 100 gm	Ghee / refined oil
½ cup / 60 gm	Onions, thinly sliced
3 tsp / 6 gm	Red chilli powder
2 tbsp / 9 gm	Coriander (dhaniya) powder
2 tsp / 12 gm	Garlic (lasan) paste
2 tsp / 12 gm	Ginger (adrak) paste
½ cup / 100 gm	Yoghurt (dahi)

2 tsp / 4 gm	Garam masala (standard, see p. 16)

Mix together:

20 / 16 gm	Almonds (badam), blanched, peeled, sliced
60 / 32 gm	Raisins (kishmish), cut into half
3 tbsp / 45 gm	Wholemilk fudge (khoya)
4 tbsp / 60 ml	Lemon (nimbu) juice
2¼ cups / 450 ml	Milk

Method:

1. Boil the rice with salt in plenty of water till cooked. Drain the excess water and keep aside.
2. Heat the ghee / oil in a wok (kadhai); add the onions and sauté until golden brown. Add the lamb, red chilli powder, coriander powder, garlic and ginger pastes, yoghurt, and salt. Cook until the lamb is well browned, adding 2 tbsp of water as and when required to avoid it sticking to the bottom of the pan. When the lamb is tender and no liquid remains add the garam masala; mix well.
3. In a greased, heavy-bottomed pan (not too large), spread a layer of rice evenly and sprinkle half the milk over it. Spread half of the lamb mixture evenly over the rice. Then cover with another layer of rice. Spread the almonds-raisins, wholemilk fudge, lemon juice mixture over this, and then spread the remaining lamb mixture. Cover with rice once again. Sprinkle with the rest of the milk.
4. Cover the dish with an aluminium foil and a lid thereafter. Put the pan on very low heat and cook on dum for half an hour.

Biryani Mutanjan
Tender lamb layered with fragrant rice

Serves: 4

Ingredients:

2 cups / 400 gm	Basmati rice, washed in a number of changes of water, soaked in enough water to cover for 30 minutes, drained	½ cup / 100 gm	Yoghurt (*dahi*)
		1 tsp / 3 gm	Sugar, dissolved over low flame, taking care not to overcook to avoid it turning bitter
Salt to taste		½ cup / 100 ml	Milk
Mix together:		2	Green cardamoms (*choti elaichi*)
700 gm	Lamb, boneless pieces		
½ tbsp / 9 gm	Garlic-ginger (*lasan-adrak*) paste	½ tsp / ½ gm	Saffron (*zafran*)
Salt to taste		2	Cinnamon (*dalchini*) sticks, 2" each
		½ tsp / 1 gm	Black cumin (*shah jeera*) seeds
½ cup / 100 gm	Ghee		
½ cup / 60 gm	Onions, sliced	½	Juice of lemon (*nimbu*)

Method:

1. Heat the ghee in a pan; add the onions and sauté until light brown. Add the lamb with the marinade. Stir to mix well and continue to cook until the water has evaporated. Reduce the heat to low and add the yoghurt and some water; cook until the lamb is tender.
2. Add the sugar syrup (do not add sugar syrup if the lamb is not tender, as it will not tenderise further) and milk; mix well. Bring the mixture to the boil and cook for a further 5 minutes.
3. Bring 3 cups water to the boil and add the drained rice, salt, green cardamoms, saffron, cinnamon sticks, black cumin seeds, and lemon juice. Stir carefully to mix. Bring back to the boil, reduce heat and cook covered until the rice is half done.
4. Layer as with other biryanis and place in a preheated oven (170°C / 325°F) for 15 minutes.

Biryani Resham
Saffron-flavoured lamb cooked with yoghurt in rice

Serves: 4-6

Ingredients:

2½ cups / 500 gm	Basmati rice, washed, soaked in water for 60 minutes
1 kg	Lamb, assorted pieces
1 cup / 200 gm	Ghee
2½ cups / 300 gm	Yoghurt (*dahi*), whisked
6 tsp / 24 gm	Salt
3 tsp / 6 gm	Red chilli powder
4 tsp / 24 gm	Ginger (*adrak*) paste
16 tsp / 24 gm	Coriander (*dhaniya*) powder
4 tsp	Black gram (*urad dal*), roasted, husked, powdered
¾ tsp	Cumin (*jeera*) powder
1 tsp / 2 gm	Black cumin (*shah jeera*) seeds, powdered
3	Black cardamoms (*badi elaichi*), powdered
15	Cloves (*laung*), powdered
½ tsp / ½ gm	Saffron (*zafran*), crushed and dissolved in 1 tbsp water

Mix together:

2 tbsp / 30 ml	Vetiver (*kewda*) essence
2¾ cups / 350 ml	Milk

Method:

1. Heat the ghee in a wok (*kadhai*); add the lamb, yoghurt, salt, red chilli powder, and ginger paste; mix well. Stir-fry until the liquid has evaporated and the lamb pieces are brown. Add just enough water, so that when the lamb is tender very little or no water remains. Add all the spices and saffron water; mix well. Lower heat and simmer until only the ghee remains.
2. Drain the rice and boil in plenty of water with the salt. When just tender, drain the rice in a flat sieve and leave to drain removing the water completely. Then spread the rice in a large tray to cool. When the rice has cooled, divide it into 4 equal parts.
3. Grease the bottom and sides of a heavy-bottomed pan with ghee. Spread one part of the rice evenly. Sprinkle the milk and vetiver mixture over the rice. Then spread half of the cooked lamb over the rice. Cover the lamb with two parts of the cooked rice and spread the remaining lamb mixture ending with a layer of rice. Cover the pan and heat until steam rises. Remove from heat and keep in a preheated oven (170°C / 325°F) for half an hour.

Shahjehani Biryani

Biryani à la cuisine royale

Serves: 12-14

Ingredients:

For the lamb:

2 kg	Lamb, deboned, cubed
½ cup / 100 gm	Ghee
¾ cup / 225 gm	Onion paste
2 tbsp / 36 gm	Ginger *(adrak)* paste
2 tbsp / 36 gm	Garlic *(lasan)* paste
1½ tbsp / 25 gm	Poppy *(khuskhus)* seed paste
12 / 12 gm	Dry red chillies *(sookhi lal mirch),* ground to a paste with water
4 tbsp / 60 gm	Almonds *(badam),* blanched, peeled, ground to a paste
3 tsp / 4½ gm	Cumin *(jeera)* powder
1½ tsp / 3 gm	Green cardamom *(choti elaichi)* seed powder
1½ tsp / 3 gm	Cinnamon *(dalchini)* powder
½ tsp / 1 gm	Nutmeg *(jaiphal)* powder
1½ tsp / 3 gm	Clove *(laung)* powder
2 tsp / 4 gm	Black pepper *(kali mirch)* powder
	Salt to taste
½ cup / 100 gm	Yoghurt *(dahi)*

For the rice:

5 cups / 1 kg	Basmati rice, washed, soaked in water for 30 minutes, drained
8 cups / 1600 ml	Water
2	Cinnamon *(dalchini)* sticks, 1" each
8	Green cardamom *(choti elaichi)* pods, cracked
1 tsp / 5 ml	Vetiver *(kewda)* essence
½ tsp / ½ gm	Saffron *(zafran)* strands, soaked in ½ cup of hot milk
¾ cup / 150 ml	Cream
1½ tsp / 2 gm	Cumin *(jeera)* seeds

For the garnishing:

2	Onions, large, sliced, fried until golden brown
½ cup / 60 gm	Raisins *(kishmish),* fried

Method:

1. **For the lamb,** heat the ghee; add the blended mixture of the pastes and spices for the lamb, stirring constantly until an aroma rises and the ghee separates. Add ½ cup water and simmer until it evaporates.
2. Add the salt. Stir and coat with the paste evenly. Cook until the lamb is well browned, adding

2 tbsp water as and when required to avoid it sticking to the bottom of the pan. Add the yoghurt and water. Cook until the lamb becomes tender and a very thick gravy remains.

3. **For the rice,** put the rice in a pan and add the water, cinnamon sticks, green cardamoms, and vetiver essence. Bring to the boil; reduce heat and cook until the rice is almost tender and the water is absorbed.

4. In a heavy, greased, ovenproof casserole, spread half the rice. Pour half of the saffron liquid, cream and black cumin seeds over it. Then spread the cooked lamb evenly. Repeat this process a second time.

5. Cover the dish tightly, pressing down with an aluminium foil. Put a lid and bake for 35 minutes in a preheated oven (170°C / 325°F).

6. Serve garnished with fried onions and raisins.

To remove the skin from garlic cloves easily, slice the cloves half down the convex side. The peels will come off easily.

Akha Jeera Champ Pulao
Cumin pilaf with mint-flavoured ribs

Serves: 6-8

Ingredients:

3 cups / 600 gm	Basmati rice, washed, soaked in water for 30 minutes, drained	1 cup / 200 gm	Butter / refined oil
		2 tsp / 4 gm	Cumin *(jeera)* seeds
1 kg	Lamb ribs, double	3	Onions, medium, sliced
5	Green cardamoms *(choti elaichi)*	1½ tsp / 3 gm	Garam masala (see p. 16)
		Make a fine paste with a little water:	
5	Cloves *(laung)*	4 tsp / 24 gm	Garlic-ginger *(lasan-adrak)* paste
4	Cinnamon *(dalchini)* sticks, 2" each	12-13 / 36 gm	Green chillies
1 tsp / 6 gm	Black peppercorns *(sabut kali mirch)*	2 tbsp / 8 gm	Green coriander *(hara dhaniya)*, fresh
Salt to taste		1 tbsp / 4 gm	Mint *(pudina)* leaves, fresh

Method:

1. Cook the ribs in 5 cups water with the green cardamoms, cloves, cinnamon sticks, black peppercorns, and salt till it is tender. Strain the stock into another pan. Keep the ribs aside.
2. Heat the butter / oil in a pan on low heat until the foam subsides. Add the cumin seeds and sauté for a few seconds. Increase the heat, add the onions and sauté till golden. Add the garam masala and the fine paste; cook until the water evaporates.
3. Add the cooked ribs and sauté, adding a few tablespoons of water. Add the stock, topping up with warm water to make 5½ cups. Bring to the rapid boil and add the rice. Stir to mix well. Lower heat and cook covered until the rice is cooked and the stock is absorbed.

(Photograph on page 4)

Korma Pulao
Aromatic rice layered with lamb

Serves: 4-6

Ingredients:

2 cups / 400 gm	Basmati rice, washed in a number of changes of water, soaked in enough water to cover for 30 minutes, drained	1 tbsp / 15 gm	Almonds (*badam*), blanched, peeled
		½ tbsp	Poppy (*khuskhus*) seeds
		½ tbsp	Sesame (*til*) seeds
600 gm	Lamb, assorted pieces	1 tsp / 2 gm	Coriander (*dhaniya*) seeds
Grind to a paste:		Salt to taste	
1 tbsp / 18 gm	Garlic (*lasan*) paste	½ tsp / 1 gm	Turmeric (*haldi*) powder
1 tbsp / 18 gm	Ginger (*adrak*) paste		
1 tsp / 2 gm	Red chilli powder	½ cup / 100 ml	Refined oil
½ tbsp / 2 gm	Coconut (*nariyal*) grated	¾ cup / 90 gm	Onions, sliced
		½ cup / 100 gm	Yoghurt (*dahi*)

Method:

1. Mix the lamb with the ground paste.
2. Heat the oil in a deep pan; add the onions and sauté till light brown. Add the lamb and mix well. Reduce heat and add yoghurt. Continue to cook until the yoghurt is absorbed and the lamb is brown in colour. Add just enough water so that very little remains when the lamb is almost tender and the oil rises to the surface. Remove the pan from the heat. Keep aside.
3. Bring 3½ cups water to the boil and then add the drained rice and salt. Stir to mix well. Bring back to the boil; reduce heat, cover and cook until the water is absorbed and the rice is almost done.
4. Grease a deep ovenproof pan. Layer the rice and lamb, beginning and ending with the rice. Spread a slightly moist cloth on the rice and cover with a tight-fitting lid. Put the pan in a preheated oven (170°C / 325°F) for 10-15 minutes.

Moplas Pulao

Spicy lamb mince in fragrant rice

Serves: 4

Ingredients:

750 gm	Lamb, minced
4 tbsp / 60 ml	Refined oil
1 cup / 120 gm	Onions, sliced
Grind together to make a fine paste:	
2½ tsp / 7½ gm	Fenugreek seeds (*methi dana*), roasted
½ tsp / 1 gm	Turmeric (*haldi*) powder
½ tsp / ¾ gm	Cumin (*jeera*) powder
¼ tsp	Black mustard seeds (*rai*)
1½ tsp / 9 gm	Ginger (*adrak*) paste
1½ tsp / 9 gm	Garlic (*lasan*) paste
Salt to taste	
1½ tsp / 7 ml	Lemon (*nimbu*) juice

1 tbsp / 15 gm	Coconut (*nariyal*), ground to a paste
2 tbsp / 8 gm	Green coriander (*hara dhaniya*), chopped
For the rice:	
2¼ cups / 450 gm	Basmati rice, washed, soaked in cold water for 30 minutes
2 tbsp / 30 ml	Refined oil
2	Bay leaves (*tej patta*)
4	Cloves (*laung*)
2	Cinnamon (*dalchini*) sticks, 2" each
¼ cup / 30 gm	Onions, sliced
Salt to taste	

Method:

1. Heat the oil in a wok (*kadhai*); add the onions and sauté until golden brown. Add the spice paste and fry until brown. Add the lamb and salt; mix well. Reduce heat and cook until the lamb is brown. Add 1 cup water and cook covered until little gravy remains. Add the lemon juice, coconut paste, and green coriander; mix well.

2. **For the rice,** heat the oil in a large pan; add the bay leaves, cloves, and cinnamon sticks. Sauté until the cloves turn dark brown. Add the onions and sauté until golden brown. Drain and add the rice. Stir to coat the rice with the oil and add 4½ cups water. Bring to the boil, lower heat and cook until the rice is tender and the water is absorbed. Mix the lamb with the rice, cover the pan and cook till steam rises. Remove the pan and keep aside for 10 minutes.

Gosht Ki Taharee

Lamb and rice cooked together in mild spices

Serves: 4

Ingredients:

2 cups / 400 gm	Basmati rice, washed in a number of changes of water, soaked in water to cover for 30 minutes, drained	1 tsp / 1½ gm	Cumin (*jeera*) powder
		¼ tsp	Turmeric (*haldi*) powder
		1 tsp / 2 gm	Red chilli powder
		½ tbsp / 12 gm	Ginger (*adrak*), chopped
250 gm	Lamb, cut into 1" cubes	½ tbsp / 12 gm	Garlic (*lasan*), chopped
½ cup / 100 ml	Refined oil		
1¼ cups / 180 gm	Onions, sliced	½ tbsp / 2 gm	Green coriander (*hara dhaniya*), chopped
Salt to taste			
Grind to a paste and mix with ¼ cup yoghurt:		2	Green chillies, slit
1 tsp / 1½ gm	Coriander (*dhaniya*) powder		

Method:

1. Heat the oil in a deep pan; add the onions and sauté until light brown. Reduce heat to low and add the yoghurt and spice mixture. Mix well and continue to fry until the yoghurt is absorbed. Add the lamb and salt. Add enough water so that all is absorbed when the lamb is tender. Cook on low heat until the lamb is tender.
2. Add the drained rice and stir slowly to mix well.
3. Add 4 cups water and bring to the boil. Reduce heat and cook until the rice is tender and fluffy and all the water is absorbed. Mix very carefully and serve garnished with green coriander and green chillies.

Sind Murgh Mussallam
Rich roasted whole chicken stuffed with rice

Serves: 4-6

Ingredients:

800-900 gm	Chicken, full, without skin	1	Onion, chopped
For the marinade:		1	Ginger (*adrak*), 1" piece, chopped
1½ tsp / 6 gm	Salt		
1 tsp / 6 gm	Bicarbonate of soda	2	Green chillies, chopped
		½ tsp / 2 gm	Salt
½ cup / 85 gm	Unsalted butter	½ tsp / 1 gm	Black pepper (*kali mirch*) powder
For the stuffing:			
½ cup / 100 gm	Rice	1	Egg, hard-boiled, chopped
2	Tomatoes, large, blanched, peeled, chopped	¼ cup / 50 gm	Yoghurt (*dahi*)
		2 tbsp / 40 gm	Butter

Method:

1. Wash the chicken and dry with kitchen paper towels, making sure that the cavity is dry as well. Keep aside.
2. **For the marinade,** rub the salt and bicarbonate of soda into the chicken; marinate for 1 hour.
3. Heat 2 tbsp unsalted butter in a large, frying pan; add the chicken and fry till golden brown. Remove and keep aside to cool.
4. **For the stuffing,** mix all the ingredients mentioned and spoon this mixture into the cavity of the chicken.
5. Place the stuffed chicken in an ovenproof dish. Dot the chicken with small portions of the unsalted butter and roast in a preheated oven (180°C / 350°F) basting regularly with butter, until the chicken becomes tender.
6. Remove the chicken from the oven and carve into serving pieces. Serve with a small amount of the stuffing, scooped out of the cavity.

Al-Roaz Al-Zirbeyan
A Saudi Arabian preparation of rice

Serves: 4-6

Ingredients:

2½ cups / 500 gm	Basmati rice, washed in a number of changes of water, soaked in enough water to cover for 30 minutes, drained	1½ cups / 300 ml	Tomato juice
		½ tsp / 1 gm	Cinnamon (*dalchini*) powder
		½ tsp / 1 gm	Black pepper (*kali mirch*) powder
1	Chicken, cut into 4 pieces	½ tsp / 1 gm	Green cardamom (*choti elaichi*) powder
½ cup / 100 ml	Refined oil	Salt to taste	
2	Onions, medium-sized, sliced into rings	2	Green chillies, chopped
		½ tsp / 1 gm	Turmeric (*haldi*) powder
½ cup / 100 gm	Yoghurt (*dahi*)		

Method:

1. Heat the oil in a wok (*kadhai*); add the onion rings and fry until golden brown. Remove with a slotted spoon and when cool crush and mix with the yoghurt. To the yoghurt and onion mixture, add tomato juice, cinnamon powder, black pepper powder, green cardamom powder, and salt.
2. In the same oil fry the chicken pieces until brown all over. Add the yoghurt mixture and the green chillies. Mix well, reduce heat and cook until the chicken is tender.
3. In another deep pan, bring 6 cups of water to the boil and then add the rice and salt. Boil until the rice is almost done. Remove the pan from the heat and drain.
4. Place half the rice in a pan. Add the turmeric powder and mix well. Spread the chicken pieces with the gravy onto the rice and then cover with the remaining rice. Pour 1 tbsp oil onto the rice and then cover the pan and cook on very low heat for half an hour.

Kibit Rus
Saudi Arabian patties stuffed with lamb

Serves: 4-6

Ingredients:

3 cups / 600 gm	Basmati rice, picked, washed
2	Potatoes, medium-sized, peeled, quartered
Salt to taste	
1 tsp / 2 gm	Turmeric (*haldi*) powder
2 tbsp / 30 gm	Tomato paste
For the filling:	
3 tbsp / 45 ml	Refined oil
¾ cup / 90 gm	Onions, minced

700 gm	Lamb, ground
1 tsp / 2 gm	Garam masala (see p. 16)
1 tsp / 2 gm	Black pepper (*kali mirch*) powder
Salt to taste	
4 tbsp / 16 gm	Parsley or Green coriander (*hara dhaniya*), chopped
Refined oil for frying	

Method:

1. Put the rice and potatoes in a deep pan and cover with boiling water. Add salt and turmeric powder and continue to boil until the rice and potatoes are tender and the water has been absorbed. Add the tomato paste and mix well. Then mince this mixture twice and keep aside.
2. **For the filling,** heat the oil in a pan; add the onions and sauté until golden brown. Add the ground lamb, garam masala, black pepper powder, and salt. Mix well, reduce heat and continue to cook until the meat is tender. Add a little water if required. Remove the pan from the heat and cool. Add the parsley or green coriander and mix well.
3. With wet hands, take a medium-sized portion of the rice and potato mix and shape into an oval, making a hollow in the centre by pushing the finger through from one end. Fill this hollow with the lamb and onion stuffing. Close the edges by pressing firmly at both ends. Repeat to make 8-10 patties.
4. Heat the oil in a wok-shaped pan. When hot, deep-fry the patties until golden brown. Remove with a slotted spoon and drain the excess oil on paper towels.

Murgh Pulao
Chicken pilaf

Serves: 4

Ingredients:

2 cups / 400 gm	Basmati rice, washed, soaked in water for 30 minutes, drained	3	Garlic *(lasan)* cloves, crushed
1	Chicken, without skin, cut into 8 pieces	4 / 12 gm	Green chillies, finely chopped
½ cup / 100 gm	Ghee / refined oil	**Mix together :**	
¾ cup / 90 gm	Onions, finely chopped	1 tsp / 2 gm	Turmeric *(haldi)* powder
1	Ginger *(adrak)*, finely chopped, 1" piece	¾ tsp / 1½ gm	Red chilli powder
		1 tbsp / 4½ gm	Coriander *(dhaniya)* powder
		¾ tsp / 1½ gm	Black pepper *(kali mirch)* powder

Method:

1. Heat the ghee / oil in a heavy-bottomed pan over moderate heat; add the onions and sauté until translucent. Then add the ginger, garlic, and green chillies; continue to fry until the mixture turns golden brown.
2. Add the chicken and increase the heat. Fry, turning them frequently, until they are golden all over. Add the spice mixture and stir, mixing them well. Cover the pan, lower heat and cook until the chicken is tender.
3. Uncover the pan, increase heat to high and stir in the rice. Mix the rice and add 3½ cups of very hot water. Cover the pan and bring to the boil. Reduce heat to low and simmer until the rice is cooked and all the liquid has been absorbed.

Ilish Bhat
Fish cooked with rice

Serves: 4

Ingredients:

2 cups / 400 gm	Basmati rice, washed in a number of changes of water, soaked in enough water to cover for 30 minutes, drained
8	Fish, hilsa or any firm white river fish, fillets
1 tsp / 2 gm	Turmeric (*haldi*) powder

Salt to taste

Mix together with a little water to make a paste:

1½ tbsp	Yellow mustard seeds (*rai*)
2	Green chillies
1 tbsp / 15 ml	Mustard (*sarson*) oil

Salt to taste

Method:

1. Rub the turmeric powder and salt on the fish and keep aside for 10 minutes. Then rub the mustard paste and lay the fish out in a round dish with a tight-fitting lid so that it can be put in the pan where the rice is being boiled for cooking.
2. Bring 4 cups water to the boil and add the rice. Bring back to the boil and then lower heat and cook covered until the rice is half cooked.
3. Place the round dish with the fish fillets in the centre of the rice, cover and cook on very low heat for another 5-6 minutes or until the rice is done.
4. Remove from heat and carefully remove the round dish.
5. Serve the cooked fish with the rice.

Cheemeem Pulao

Prawn pilaf

Serves: 4-6

Ingredients:

2½ cups / 500 gm	Basmati rice, washed in a number of changes of water, soaked in water to cover for 30 minutes, drained	½ cup / 100 gm	Yoghurt (*dahi*)
		½ cup / 50 gm	Coconut (*nariyal*), grated
		½ cup / 100 ml	Coconut milk (*nariyal ka doodh*)
400 gm	Prawns, peeled, deveined, washed and pat dried	Salt to taste	
¼ cup / 50 ml	Refined oil	15	Cloves (*laung*)
Grind to a paste with ¼ cup water:		2	Cinnamon (*dalchini*) sticks, 2" each
1	Ginger (*adrak*), 1" piece, peeled, chopped	5	Green cardamoms (*choti elaichi*)
6	Green chillies, chopped	Salt to taste	
8	Garlic (*lasan*) cloves	1¾ tbsp / 25 gm	Cashew nuts (*kaju*), fried until golden brown
1½ tsp / 2 gm	Cumin (*jeera*) powder	1 cup / 120 gm	Onions, sliced, fried until golden brown
¾ cup	Tomatoes, chopped		

Method:

1. Heat the oil in a deep pan; add the ginger, green chilli-garlic paste, and cumin powder; sauté until the water evaporates. Add the tomatoes and sauté until they soften and darken in colour. Add the yoghurt. Stir to mix well and continue to cook until the yoghurt is absorbed and the oil rises to the surface.

2. Add the coconut and then a few seconds later add the coconut milk and salt. Stir to mix well and continue to cook until the gravy thickens. Add the prawns and bring to the boil. Turn off the heat. Pour the prawns with the sauce into an ovenproof pan. Keep aside.

3. Bring 5-6 cups of water to a rapid boil. Add the cloves, cinnamon sticks, green cardamoms,

and salt. Add the rice and boil for 6-7 minutes. Drain the rice and spread it on top of the prawns. Spread the cashew nuts and fried onions. Make a few wells in the rice all the way to the bottom to allow the steam to escape.

4. Cover the pan with an aluminium foil and then with a tight-fitting lid. Put the pan in a preheated oven (170°C / 325°F) for 15 minutes. Mix before serving.

While making a mixed vegetable salad, cut the tomatoes in vertical slices; they will drip less.

Dewanee Khitchree
A delightful blend of rice and pulses

Serves: 4

Ingredients:

¼ cup / 37 gm	Green gram whole (*moong*), picked, washed		soaked in enough water to cover for 30 minutes, drained
¼ cup / 27 gm	Lentil (*masoor dal*), picked, washed	½ cup / 100 ml	Refined oil
¼ cup / 40 gm	Split red gram (*arhar dal*), picked, washed	1½ tsp / 6 gm	Salt
		½ tsp / 1 gm	Turmeric (*haldi*) powder
¼ cup / 40 gm	Bengal gram (*chana dal*), picked, washed	½ tsp / 1 gm	Red chilli powder
		½ tbsp / 9 gm	Ginger (*adrak*) paste
2 cups / 400 gm	Basmati rice, washed in a number of changes of water,	½ tbsp / 9 gm	Garlic (*lasan*) paste

Method:

1. Heat the refined oil in a deep pan; add the green gram, lentil, split red gram, and Bengal gram; stir to mix well. Reduce heat and stir-fry for 5-7 minutes. Add 1 cup water and bring to the boil. Cook until the mixture is tender.
2. Add the salt, turmeric powder, red chilli powder, ginger and garlic pastes; mix well. Add the drained rice and stir to mix well with the cooked grams.
3. Add 3½ cups water and bring to the boil. Reduce heat and cook until the rice is tender and the water is absorbed.
4. Cover with a tight lid and keep in a preheated oven (170°C / 325°F) for 10 minutes.

(Photograph on page 6)

Mughlai Khitchree
Rice cooked with green gram

Serves: 2-4

Ingredients:

1 cup / 200 gm	Basmati rice	3	Cloves (*laung*)
½ cup / 75 gm	Green gram (*moong dal*)	3	Green cardamoms (*choti elaichi*)
2½ tbsp / 37 gm	Ghee		
1	Bay leaf (*tej patta*)	1	Cinnamon (*dalchini*) stick, 1" piece
Grind to a coarse paste:			
¼ cup / 30 gm	Onions, chopped		
3	Green chillies	15	Curry leaves (*kadhi patta*)
1 tsp / 6 gm	Ginger (*adrak*) paste	Salt to taste	
½ tsp / 3 gm	Garlic (*lasan*) paste	12	Cashew nuts (*kaju*), fried until golden
Grind to a fine powder:			
½ tsp	Black cumin (*shah jeera*) seeds		

Method:

1. Wash the rice and green gram in a number of changes of water and then soak in enough water to cover for 30 minutes and then drain.
2. Heat the ghee in a deep pan; add the bay leaf. When it changes colour add the onion paste. Sauté until the paste is golden brown.
3. Add the spice powder, and curry leaves; mix well. Add 3 cups water and bring to the boil. Add the rice, green gram, and salt. Bring back to the boil and reduce heat to medium and cook until the rice and gram are tender.
4. Serve garnished with cashew nuts.

Kabooli
Chickpea rice

Serves: 4

Ingredients:

2 cups / 400 gm	Basmati rice, washed in a number of changes of water, soaked in water to cover for 30 minutes, drained	1 tbsp / 6 gm	Cumin (*jeera*) seeds
		3	Green cardamoms (*choti elaichi*), seeds only
¾ cup / 112 gm	Dried chickpeas (*kabooli chana*), boiled in 1½ cups of water until soft, drained	4	Green chillies, finely chopped
		1 tbsp / 4 gm	Mint (*pudina*) leaves, finely chopped
½ cup / 100 ml	Refined oil	1 tbsp / 4 gm	Green coriander (*hara dhaniya*), finely chopped
½ cup / 60 gm	Onions, sliced		
½ cup / 100 gm	Yoghurt (*dahi*)	½ tsp / 1 gm	Garam masala (standard, see p. 16)
1 tsp / 6 gm	Ginger (*adrak*) paste	¼ cup / 50 ml	Milk
1 tsp / 6 gm	Garlic (*lasan*) paste	2 tbsp / 30 ml	Lemon (*nimbu*) juice

Method:

1. Heat the oil in a pan; add the onions and sauté until brown. Reduce heat and add the yoghurt, ginger and garlic pastes, cumin and green cardamom seeds, green chillies, mint leaves, green coriander, garam masala, and salt. Mix well and continue to cook until the yoghurt is absorbed. Add the chickpeas to the spice mixture; mix well. Cook on simmer for 5-7 minutes.
2. Bring 5 cups water to the boil in a deep pan. Add the rice and ½ tbsp salt; boil until the rice is more than half done. Remove from the heat and drain the the excess water. Transfer rice onto a tray to cool.
3. In an ovenproof casserole spread ½ the rice. Cover with a layer of chickpeas. Sprinkle the milk over and then cover with the remaining rice. Sprinkle lemon juice and cover the casserole tightly first with an aluminium foil and then with a lid. Put the casserole in a preheated oven (170°C / 325°F) for 30 minutes.

Marwari Gatta Pulao
Steamed gram flour rolls in rice

Serves: 4

Ingredients:

For the *gatta* (steamed gram flour rolls):

1 cup / 100 gm	Bengal gram flour (*besan*)
¼ tsp	Bicarbonate of soda
2 tsp / 3 gm	Coriander (*dhaniya*) powder
2 tsp / 4 gm	Red chilli powder
1 tsp / 2 gm	Garam masala (standard, see p. 16)
Salt to taste	
2 tbsp / 30 ml	Refined oil
2 tsp	Yoghurt (*dahi*)
Refined oil for frying	
4 cups/800 ml	Water for boiling the *gattas*

For the rice:

1½ cups / 300 gm	Basmati rice, washed in a

	number of changes of water, soaked in water to cover for 30 minutes, drained
3 tbsp / 45 gm	Ghee
4	Cloves (*laung*)
1	Cinnamon (*dalchini*) stick, 1" piece
4	Green cardamoms (*choti elaichi*)
5 tsp / 10 gm	Turmeric (*haldi*) powder
Salt to taste	

For the garnishing:

1 tbsp / 10 gm	Raisins (*kishmish*), fried
10	Cashew nuts (*kaju*), fried

Method:

1. **For the *gatta*,** mix the first 6 ingredients well; add the oil and rub with fingers until well incorporated. Add a little water and knead into a stiff dough. Divide the dough into three equal portions. Make each portion into a ½" thick × 4" -long roll.
2. Boil the *gatta* rolls in a large pan and on high heat, uncovered, for 10-12 minutes. Remove, drain and cool. Cut each roll into ½"-long pieces and deep-fry the *gattas* until light brown.
3. **For the rice,** heat the ghee in a pan; add the whole spices and sauté until the cardamoms change colour. Add the drained rice and stir to coat the grains with the ghee. Add turmeric powder, salt, and 3 cups water. Bring to the boil. Lower heat, cover and cook until the rice is half done. Add the fried *gattas* and continue to cook until the rice is done.
4. Garnish with raisins and cashew nuts.

Kanegach Yakhnee Pulao
Mushroom in rice – cooked Kashmiri-style

Serves: 4-6

Ingredients:

1½ cups / 300 gm	Basmati rice, washed in a number of changes of water, soaked in enough water to cover for 30 minutes, drained	10	Cloves (*laung*)
		4	Cinnamon (*dalchini*) sticks, 1" each
		Salt to taste	
1 kg	Mushrooms (*gucchi*), cut into 4 pieces each, washed	1 tsp / 6 gm	Garlic (*lasan*), ground
		1 cup / 200 gm	Cooked yoghurt (see p. 17)
½ cup / 100 ml	Refined oil	1½ tsp / 3 gm	Dry ginger powder (*sonth*)
¼ cup / 75 gm	Onion paste	1½ tsp / 2 gm	Coriander (*dhaniya*) powder
10	Green cardamoms (*choti elaichi*)	¼ tsp	Black cumin (*shah jeera*) seeds
4	Black cardamoms (*badi elaichi*)	¼ tsp	Black pepper (*kali mirch*) powder
		¼ tsp	Dry mint (*pudina*) leaves

Method:

1. Boil the mushrooms in water for 5-7 minutes. Drain, wash in cold water and drain.
2. Put the washed mushrooms in a pan and add the oil, onion paste, green and black cardamoms, cloves, cinnamon sticks, salt, and garlic. Put the pan on heat and mix well. Stir and cook until the mushrooms are light brown in colour.
3. Add the cooked yoghurt and continue to cook until the oil separates. Add 3 cups water, dry ginger and coriander powder. Stir to mix well. Add the drained rice. Stir. Bring to the boil, reduce heat and simmer until the rice is done.
4. Garnish with black cumin seeds, black pepper powder, and dry mint leaves.

Til Aur Curry Patta Bhat
Rice seasoned with sesame seeds

Serves: 4

Ingredients:

2 cups / 400 gm	Basmati rice, cleaned, soaked in water for 1 hour, drained	18	Curry leaves *(kadhi patta)*
		1 tsp / 3 gm	Mustard seeds *(rai)*
		1 tsp / 2 gm	Cumin *(jeera)* seeds
3½ cups / 700 ml	Water	¾ cup	Sesame *(til)* seeds
2 tsp / 8 gm	Salt	2 tbsp / 30 ml	Lemon *(nimbu)* juice
3 tbsp / 45 ml	Sesame *(til)* oil		

Method:

1. Put the drained rice, water, and salt in a heavy pan. Bring to the boil. Reduce heat, cover the pan with a lid and cook until the rice is cooked and the water is absorbed. Keep warm and put aside.
2. Heat the sesame oil in a saucepan; add the curry leaves, mustard seeds, and cumin seeds. Sauté until the leaves change colour and the mustard and cumin seeds crackle. Reduce heat and add sesame seeds; sauté until they are evenly golden brown.
3. Add this seasoning with the lemon juice to the cooked rice. Mix well, taking care that the rice grains do not break.

Pudina Aur Dhaniya Chawal
Mint and coriander-flavoured rice

Serves: 4-6

Ingredients:

2 cups / 400 gm	Basmati rice, washed, soaked in water for 30 minutes, drained	1½ cups / 300 gm	Yoghurt (dahi), whisked
½ tsp / ½ gm	Saffron (zafran)	1	Onion, large, finely chopped
½ cup / 100 gm	Ghee / refined oil	3 tbsp / 12 gm	Green coriander (hara dhaniya), finely chopped
1	Cinnamon (dalchini) stick, 2" piece	1 tbsp / 4 gm	Mint (pudina) leaves, finely chopped
4	Cloves (laung)	2 tsp / 4 gm	White pepper (safed mirch) powder
2 tsp / 12 gm	Ginger (adrak), minced	Salt to taste	

Method:

1. Put the drained rice in a pan and add water to just about cover it. Add saffron and boil for 10 minutes. Remove from heat and drain all the excess water. Keep aside.
2. Heat the ghee / oil in a wok (kadhai); add the cinnamon stick and cloves. Sauté until they crackle. Add the ginger and stir. Add the drained rice and stir until it is well coated with the oil. Add the yoghurt, onion, green coriander, mint leaves, white pepper powder, and salt. Cook, covered, on very low heat until the rice is cooked and the yoghurt is absorbed.

Mattarwale Chawal
Pea pilaf

Serves 4

Ingredients:

1½ cups / 300 gm	Basmati rice, washed, soaked in water for 1 hour, drained	1 tsp / 2 gm	Garam masala (fragrant, see p. 17)
1½ cups / 200 gm	Green peas *(mattar),* shelled	Salt to taste	
2 tbsp / 30 gm	Ghee	1 cup / 120 gm	Onions, sliced, fried golden brown
1 tsp / 2 gm	Cumin *(jeera)* seeds		
1 cup / 120 gm	Onions, finely sliced		

Method:

1. Heat the ghee in a wok (*kadhai*); add the cumin seeds. When they crackle, add the onions and sauté until golden. Add the garam masala, stir and add the rice. Sauté for 2 minutes, until the rice is well coated with ghee.
2. Add 3 cups water and bring to the boil. Reduce heat, add the green peas and salt; stir. Cover and cook until all the water is absorbed and the rice and peas are done. Garnish with fried onions.

Nariyal Bhat
Coconut-milk rice

Serves: 4

Ingredients:

2 cups / 400 gm	Basmati rice, washed, soaked in water for 30 minutes, drained	10	Curry leaves *(kadhi patta)*
		6	Green cardamoms *(choti elaichi)*
3 tbsp / 45 gm	Ghee / refined oil	6	Cloves *(laung)*
1 cup / 120 gm	Onions, sliced	4 cups / 800 ml	Coconut milk *(nariyal ka doodh)*, thick
10	Black peppercorns *(sabut kali mirch)*		Salt to taste

Method:

1. Heat the ghee / oil in a wok (*kadhai*); add the onions, black peppercorns, curry leaves, green cardamoms, and cloves. Sauté together until the onions turn golden brown.
2. Add the rice and stir until it is evenly coated with ghee / oil. Add the coconut milk and salt. Cook until the rice is tender.

Chitrannam
Lemon rice

Serves: 2-4

Ingredients:

1½ cups / 300 gm	Rice, long-grained, washed and soaked in water for 30 minutes	2 tbsp / 30 gm	Cashew nuts (*kaju*), split, raw, roasted
1 tbsp / 15 ml	Refined oil	1 tsp	Black gram (*urad dal*), husked
½ tsp / 1½ gm	Yellow mustard seeds (*rai*)	1 tsp	Split Bengal gram (*chana dal*), roasted
½ tsp / 1½ gm	Black mustard seeds (*rai*)		
a pinch	Asafoetida (*hing*) powder	¾ tsp	Turmeric (*haldi*) powder
25	Curry leaves (*kadhi patta*)	2½ tbsp / 37 ml	Lemon (*nimbu*) juice
½ tsp / 3 gm	Ginger (*adrak*), chopped		Salt to taste
1	Green chilli, chopped	2 tbsp / 30 ml	Water
3	Dry red chillies (*sookhi lal mirch*), shredded thickly	1 tbsp / 4 gm	Green coriander (*hara dhaniya*), chopped

Method:

1. Drain the rice and boil in 4 cups water until the rice is just tender. Drain the rice thoroughly, of all the excess water. Keep aside in a warm oven.
2. Heat the oil in a pan; add both the yellow and black mustard seeds. When they pop, add the asafoetida, curry leaves, ginger, green chilli, dry red chillies, cashew nuts, husked black gram, Bengal gram, and turmeric powder. Sauté for a few seconds. Add the lemon juice, salt and water. Stir-fry for a minute.
3. Toss this tempering into the rice and mix carefully. Garnish with green coriander.

Thengai Sadam
Coconut rice

Serves: 2-4

Ingredients:

1½ cups / 300 gm	Basmati rice, washed, soaked in water for 30 minutes, drained	1 tsp / 3 gm	Garlic (*lasan*), finely chopped
		1 tsp	Black gram (*urad dal*), husked
3 tbsp / 45 ml	Refined oil	2 tbsp / 50 gm	Split Bengal gram (*chana dal*)
1 tsp / 3 gm	Black mustard seeds (rai)	25	Curry leaves (*kadhi patta*)
4	Dry red chillies (*sookhi lal mirch*), shredded	¼ tsp	Turmeric (*haldi*) powder
		a pinch	Asafoetida (*hing*) powder
2	Green chillies, sliced	Salt to taste	
¾ tsp / 4½ gm	Ginger (*adrak*), finely chopped	¾ cup / 75 gm	Coconut (*nariyal*), grated, roasted until golden brown

Method:

1. Boil the rice in 4 cups water for 5 minutes. Drain well and spread on a tray to cool. Keep aside.
2. Heat the oil in a pan; sauté the mustard seeds, dry red chillies, green chillies, ginger, and garlic for a minute. Add the black gram, Bengal gram, curry leaves, and turmeric powder. Sauté until the grams are golden in colour. Add the asafoetida, salt, and roasted coconut. Add the boiled rice and mix carefully so as not to break the grains.
3. Remove the pan from the heat and keep aside for 1 hour to allow the flavours to penetrate. Reheat and serve.

Kullum
Cabbage rice

Serves: 2-4

Ingredients:

1¼ cups / 250 gm	Basmati rice, washed, soaked for 30 minutes, drained	¾ cup / 90 gm	Onions, sliced
2 cups	Cabbage (*bandh gobi*), finely shredded	½ tsp / 1½ gm	Black mustard seeds (*rai*)
		12	Curry leaves (*kadhi patta*)
		3	Green chillies, chopped
1 tbsp	Salt	1½ tsp / 3 gm	Garam masala (see p. 16)
5 tbsp / 75 ml	Refined oil	Salt to taste	

Method:

1. Bring 3½ cups water to the boil. Add the rice and salt; mix well. Bring back to the boil and reduce heat to medium. Cover and cook until the rice is tender and fluffy. Drain the excess water and keep the rice aside in a warm place.
2. Heat the oil in a deep pan; add the onions. Sauté until golden brown. Remove the onions with a slotted spoon and drain on paper towels.
3. In the same oil, add the black mustard seeds, curry leaves, and green chillies. Sauté until the seeds pop. Add the garam masala and stir. Add the cabbage leaves. Sauté for 2 minutes. Add ¼ cup water and salt to taste. Reduce heat, cover and cook until the water has evaporated. Remove from heat and keep aside.
4. To assemble, place the fried onions on the base of a large saucepan. Spread a layer of cooked rice and then the cabbage ending with the remaining rice. Cover the pan with a tight lid and cook on very low heat for 10 minutes. Mix carefully and serve.

Narangi Ni Chawal
Orange rice

Serves: 2-4

Ingredients:

1¼ cups / 250 gm	Rice, washed, soaked in water for 20 minutes, drained	1 cup / 120 gm	Onions, sliced
2	Oranges (*narangi*), cut in half	6	Cloves (*laung*)
¼ tsp / ¼ gm	Saffron (*zafran*), pounded, mixed with ¼ cup hot milk	2	Bay leaves (*tej patta*)
		1 tsp / 2 gm	Black cumin (*shah jeera*) seeds
2 tbsp / 30 ml	Refined oil	1	Grated rind and juice of lemon (*nimbu*)

Method:

1. Squeeze and collect the juice of the oranges. Remove the pulp and discard. Boil the skins in water for 5 minutes. Remove and cool. When cool remove the white pith and shred the skins finely. Keep aside.
2. Bring 3 lt water to the boil. Add 3 tsp salt. Add the drained rice and bring back to the boil. Reduce heat and boil for a further 5-6 minutes, until the rice is ¾ cooked. Drain the rice and mix half of it with the saffron milk.
3. Heat the oil in a pan; add the onions, cloves, and bay leaves. Sauté until the onions are golden brown. Remove with a slotted spoon and drain the excess oil on paper towels.
4. Now in a large saucepan first add the oil then the plain rice. Sprinkle the lemon rind and half of the fried onions and spices. Add ½ tsp salt and then the saffron rice. Add the shredded orange peel and the remaining onions.
5. Make a few holes down through the rice and sprinkle the lemon and orange juice and another ½ tsp of salt.
6. Cover the rice with a moist paper towel and a tight lid. Cook on very low heat for 10 minutes. Mix carefully and serve.

Rangila Pulao
Tri-coloured rice

Serves: 4

Rice as Accompaniment

Ingredients:

2 cups / 400 gm	Basmati rice, washed, soaked in cold water for 30 minutes, drained	4	Cloves (*laung*)
2 tbsp / 30 ml	Refined oil	4	Green cardamoms (*choti elaichi*)
¾ cup / 90 gm	Onions, finely sliced	Salt to taste	
2	Cinnamon (*dalchini*) sticks, 2" each	a few drops	Red and green food colouring
		1	Carrot (*gajar*), sliced
		1	Tomato, sliced

Method:

1. Heat the oil in a pan; add the onions, cinnamon sticks, cloves, and green cardamoms. Sauté until the onions are golden brown.
2. Add the drained rice and stir carefully coating the rice grains with the oil.
3. Add 4 cups of hot water and the salt. Stir well and bring to the boil. Reduce heat to low, cover the pan and cook until the water is absorbed and the rice is tender and fluffy.
4. Remove the pan from the heat and take ½ cup of cooked rice and mix with bright red colour and mix another ½ cup of rice with some bright green colour. Arrange the rice in three different colours and garnish with tomato and carrot.

Tamatar Palak Bhat
Tomato and spinach rice

Serves: 4

Ingredients:

2 cups / 400 gm	Basmati rice, washed, soaked in enough water to cover for 30 minutes, drained
¼ cup / 50 ml	Refined oil
¼ cup / 30 gm	Onions, thinly sliced
1 cup	Tomatoes, finely chopped
275 gm	Spinach (*palak*), washed, finely chopped. Cook in ½ cup water until tender and no water remains
¼ tsp	Turmeric (*haldi*) powder
1 tsp / 2 gm	Coriander (*dhaniya*) seeds, roasted, powdered
1 tsp / 2 gm	Cumin (*jeera*) seeds, roasted, powdered
Salt to taste	

Method:

1. Heat the oil in a heavy-bottomed pan; add the onions and sauté until brown. Add the drained rice and stir carefully to coat the rice grain with the oil.
2. Add the tomatoes, cooked spinach, turmeric powder, coriander powder, cumin powder, and salt. Stir carefully to mix well and heat through.
3. Add 3 cups water and bring to the boil. Cover the pan with a tight lid and reduce heat to very low. Continue to cook for 20-23 minutes. Remove cover and stir the rice gently. Continue to cook for another 7-10 minutes on very low heat. Remove and serve.

Parsi Dhansak Pulao

Fragrant rice cooked in Parsi style

Serves: 4

Ingredients:

1½ cups / 300 gm	Basmati rice, washed in a number of changes of water, soaked in enough water to cover for 30 minutes, drained	6	Cloves (*laung*)
		3	Green cardamoms (*choti elaichi*)
		8	Black peppercorns (*sabut kali mirch*)
3 tbsp / 45 ml	Refined oil	1 cup / 120 gm	Onions, sliced
2	Cinnamon (*dalchini*) sticks, 1" each	2 tbsp / 40 gm	Sugar
		Salt to taste	

Method:

1. Heat the oil in a pan; add the cinnamon sticks, cloves, green cardamoms, and black peppercorns. Sauté until the green cardamoms change colour. Add the onions and sauté until light brown. Add the drained rice and stir carefully for 3 minutes.
2. Dissolve the sugar in a pan over very low heat until it is golden. Remove the pan from the heat and add ½ cup water; stir to mix well. Return the pan to the heat and bring back to the boil.
3. Add the sugar water, 2½ cups water, and salt. Bring to the boil and then reduce heat and cook covered until the rice is done and the water is absorbed completely.

Maharashtrian Masala Bhat

Spicy Maharashtrian rice

Serves: 4

Ingredients:

1½ cups / 300 gm	Basmati rice, washed in a number of changes of water, soaked in enough water to cover for 10 minutes, drained	½ tsp / 1 gm	Cumin (*jeera*) seeds
		½ tsp / 1 gm	Black cumin (*shah jeera*) seeds
5 tbsp / 75 ml	Refined oil	1 tsp / 3 gm	Sesame (*til*) seeds
¾ tsp	Black mustard seeds (*rai*)	1 tsp / 2 gm	Garam masala (fragrant, see p.17)
5	Green chillies, slit		
1 tsp / 2 gm	Turmeric (*haldi*) powder	1½ tsp / 3 gm	Red chilli powder
8-10	Gherkins (*tindli*), small sized, cut into 4 slices each	1½ tsp / 7 ml	Lemon (*nimbu*) juice
		Salt to taste	
¾ cup	Green peas (*mattar*), shelled	**For the garnishing:**	
Dry roast and grind to a fine powder:		10	Cashew nuts (*kaju*), lightly fried
1 tsp / 2 gm	Coriander (*dhaniya*) seeds	2 tbsp / 20 gm	Raisins (*kishmish*), sliced
1	Cinnamon (*dalchini*) stick, 1" piece	8-10	Coconut (*nariyal*), cut into slices

Method:

1. Heat the oil in a pan; add the mustard seeds. When they splutter, add the green chillies and turmeric powder; stir and add the gherkins and green peas. Lower heat and continue to cook for 2 minutes. Add the drained rice and mix carefully to coat the grain with the oil, and continue to fry until all the water has evaporated.
2. Add the roasted powder, garam masala, and red chilli powder. Stir to mix well. Add 3 cups water, lemon juice, and salt. Increase heat and bring to the boil. Reduce heat and cook covered until the water is absorbed and the rice is done.
3. Garnish with cashew nuts, raisins and coconut.

Kashmiri Palow
Fragrant Kashmiri rice

Serves: 4-6

Ingredients:

3 cups / 600 gm	Basmati rice, washed	2½ tbsp / 10 gm	Fennel (*moti saunf*) seeds
For the stock:		Salt to taste	
15 cups / 3 lt	Water	1½ cups / 180 gm	Onions, sliced, fried until brown, drained
6	Large bones from the leg of lamb		
5	Bay leaves (*tej patta*)	¾ tbsp / 4½ gm	Black cumin (*kala jeera*) seeds
15	Black cardamoms (*badi elaichi*)	7	Green cardamoms (*choti elaichi*)
4	Cinnamon (*dalchini*) sticks, 2" each	½ cup / 100 gm	Ghee

Method:

1. **For the stock,** bring all the ingredients (except the onion) to the boil in a deep pan. Lower heat, cover and continue to boil for 15-18 minutes. Now add the browned onions and boil for another 5 minutes. Remove from heat and keep aside to cool. Strain the stock through a muslin cloth to get 7 cups stock. Add more water, if required.
2. Bring the strained stock to the boil in a deep pan; add the rice, black cumin seeds, and green cardamoms. Bring the mixture back to the boil, then reduce heat and cook until the rice is ¾ done.
3. Heat the ghee in another pan; pour in the rice mixture. Cover the pan with a tight lid and cook on very low heat until the rice is just right.

Chawal Ka Cheela
Spicy rice flour pancakes

Serves: 4-6

Ingredients:

2 cups / 230 gm	Rice flour		½ tsp	Carom (*ajwain*) seeds (optional)
1 tsp / 6 gm	Garlic (*lasan*), ground		Salt to taste	
1 tsp / 6 gm	Ginger (*adrak*), ground		4	Green chillies, finely chopped
1 tsp / 2 gm	Red chilli powder		Ghee for frying	

Method:

1. Mix all the ingredients together except ghee. Add enough water to make a smooth pancake-like batter.
2. Heat 1 tbsp ghee on a flat pan; pour one ladleful of the batter and spread the batter into a disc with the back of the ladle. Fry until light brown and then flip over and do the same. Remove and repeat until all the batter is consumed.

Uttapum
Black gram and rice pancakes flavoured with coconut

Serves: 4-6

Ingredients:

1 cup / 200 gm	Basmati rice, washed, soaked in water for 12 hours	4	Green chillies, chopped
½ cup / 75 gm	Split black gram (*urad dal*), without skin, washed, soaked in water for 12 hours	¼ cup / 30 gm	Onion, grated
		2 tbsp / 8 gm	Green coriander (*hara dhaniya*), finely chopped
2 tbsp / 60 gm	Yoghurt (*dahi*)	2 tbsp / 8 gm	Coconut (*nariyal*), grated
1 tsp / 6 gm	Bicarbonate of soda		Salt to taste
			Refined oil for frying

Method:

1. Wash the soaked rice and then grind to a smooth paste. Keep aside. Then wash the split black gram and also grind to a paste. (Add a little water while grinding, as the pastes should be of a thick consistency).
2. Add the yoghurt and bicarbonate of soda; beat well until the batter is light and frothy. Add the green chillies, onion, green coriander, coconut, and salt. Mix well and keep the batter aside for 20-25 minutes.
3. Heat 1 tsp oil on a flat pan; pour 2 tbsp of the batter. Spread out with the back of a spoon into a thick disc of 2" diameter. Fry on low heat until small bubbles appear on the surface. Turn over and cook the other side until crisp and golden. Remove and repeat till all the batter is consumed.

Coorgi Roti
Shallow-fried rice flour bread

Serves: 4-6

Ingredients:

2 cups / 230 gm	Rice flour	ground with a little water to
Salt to taste		make a smooth purée
1½ cups / 300 gm	Basmati rice, well cooked,	Ghee for shallow-frying

Method:

1. Sift the rice flour and salt together in a bowl. Add the rice purée and a little water if required to make smooth pliable dough.
2. Divide the dough into 10 equal balls. Roll out each ball into a 6" disc which is ⅙" thick.
3. Heat the ghee on a flat pan; place the disc flat on it and fry making sure that dark brown specks do not appear on the underside. Turn the disc over and pour some ghee from the side to shallow-fry. Remove and repeat till all the discs are fried.

Phirni
Ground rice dessert flavoured with saffron

Serves: 4-6

Ingredients:

3 cups / 600 ml	Milk	½ tsp / 1 gm	Green cardamom *(choti elaichi)* seeds , ground
3 tbsp	Rice, ground		
6 tbsp / 80 gm	Sugar	a pinch	Saffron *(zafran)*
1 tbsp / 15 ml	Vetiver *(kewda)* essence	a few	Raisins *(kishmish)*

Method:

1. Mix 4 tbsp milk with the ground rice and make a smooth paste. Keep aside. Bring the rest of the milk to the boil and add the sugar, stirring until the sugar dissolves completely.
2. Remove the pan from the heat and add the ground rice paste. Stir well and return to heat. Stir constantly until the mixture thickens. Boil for 5 minutes, stirring. Remove the pan from the heat. Add the vetiver essence and green cardamom powder; mix well.
3. Pour the mixture into individual dessert bowls and garnish with saffron and raisins. Chill and serve.

Kheer
Sweetened rice pudding

Serves: 4-6

Ingredients:

1 cup / 200 gm	Basmati rice, soaked in plenty of water for 30 minutes, washed, drained	½ cup / 50 gm	Raisins *(kishmish)*, soaked in water for 30 minutes, drained
10 cups / 2 lt	Milk	400 gm	Condensed milk
5	Green cardamoms *(choti elaichi)*, cracked	½ cup / 60 gm	Almonds *(badam)*, blanched, peeled, sliced

Method:

1. Bring the milk to the boil. Add the rice and the green cardamoms. Cook, stirring continuously, until the milk is fully absorbed and the rice is tender and broken.
2. Add the raisins and condensed milk. Cook, stirring regularly until the consistency is thick, and the mixture sticks to the ladle. Garnish with almonds. Refrigerate and serve chilled.

Mewa Ka Zarda
Rice pudding enriched with dried fruits

Serves: 4-6

Ingredients:

2 cups / 400 gm	Basmati rice, picked, washed, soaked in water for 1 hour, drained	½ cup / 50 gm	Charoli seeds (*chironji*), coarsely ground
1 cup / 200 ml	Refined oil	20 / 16 gm	Almonds (*badam*), blanched, peeled, sliced
4 cups / 800 ml	Milk	20 / 25 gm	Cashew nuts (*kaju*), sliced
1½ tsp / 3 gm	Green cardamom (*choti elaichi*) seeds, powdered	¼ cup / 30 gm	Raisins (*kishmish*), soaked in water for 15 minutes, drained
¼ tsp / ½ gm	Nutmeg (*jaiphal*) powder		
¼ tsp / ½ gm	Mace (*javitri*) powder	2½ cups / 375 gm	Sugar
½ tsp / ½ gm	Saffron (*zafran*), soaked in 2 tbsp hot milk		

Method:

1. Heat the oil in a deep pan; when hot, add the drained rice. Stir and add the milk. Stir to mix well. Cover the rice until it is cooked and the milk is fully absorbed.
2. Mix the green cardamom, nutmeg and mace powders with the saffron milk.
3. Add the saffron mixture, charoli seeds, almonds, cashew nuts, raisins, and sugar to the rice. Mix well.
4. Cover the pan with a tight lid and put in a preheated oven (100°C / 212°F) for 10-12 minutes.

Gujbhata
Sweetened rice mixed with grated carrots

Serves: 4-6

Ingredients:

2 cups / 400 gm	Basmati rice, washed in a number of changes of water, soaked in enough water to cover for 30 minutes, drained	6	Green cardamoms (*choti elaichi*)
		6	Cloves (*laung*)
		2 cups / 300 gm	Sugar
		4 cups	Carrots (*gajar*), grated
¼ cup / 50 gm	Ghee	½ tsp / 2½ ml	Vetiver (*kewda*) essence

Method:

1. Bring 6 cups water to the boil. Add the drained rice and cook uncovered until the rice is half done. Drain the rice and keep aside.
2. Heat the ghee in a pan; add the green cardamoms and cloves; sauté until the cardamoms change colour. Add the sugar, carrots, rice, and vetiver essence; stir carefully to mix well.
3. Reduce heat to very low. Cover and cook until the carrots are very tender and the rice is cooked, stirring occasionally.

INDEX